J   575849
796.2   12.95
Ita
Italia
In-line skating

DATE DUE			
AU25'95			

GREAT RIVER REGIONAL LIBRARY

St. Cloud, Minnesota 56301

Action Sports Library

In-Line Skating

Bob Italia

Published by Abdo & Daughters, 6535 Cecilia Circle, Edina, Minnesota 55439.

Library bound edition distributed by Rockbottom Books, Pentagon Tower, P.O. Box 36036, Minneapolis, Minnesota 55435.

Printed in the United States.

ISBN: 1-56239-076-7

Library of Congress Card Catalog Number: 91-073021

Cover Photos: ©ALLSPORT USA/PHOTOGRAPHER, 1991.
Inside Photos: ©ALLSPORT USA/PHOTOGRAPHER, 1991.

Warning: The series *Action Sports Library* is intended as entertainment for children. These sporting activities should never be attempted without the proper conditioning, training, instruction, supervision, and equipment.

Edited by Rosemary Wallner

CONTENTS

In-line skating—the hottest sport on wheels!

IN-LINE SKATING

A Popular Action Sport

They look clumsy and uncomfortable—a cross between hockey skates and roller skates. But when you strap them on, they become the smoothest things on wheels. Hockey star Wayne Gretzky and his wife Janet Jones have been seen on them. So has actor Michael J. Fox. They're part of the hottest action sports around—in-line skating!

It All Started in Minnesota

In-line skates are not ordinary roller skates. Typical roller skates have two sets of side-by-side wheels. All four wheels on in-line skates are aligned one behind the other in a single line. This single line of wheels makes the in-line skates run smoother and faster—and makes maneuvering much easier. The in-line blades are attached to boots that are made of molded polyurethane (plastic) and have a padded liner.

In-line skates were developed in 1979 by Brennan and Scott Olson. These two brothers played hockey in the winter. But when summer came, the only ice that could be found was in indoor skating rinks. How could they train for hockey and enjoy the warm weather at the same time?

One day at a rummage sale, the Olson's found an old pair of ice skates with wheels attached in a straight line. They made some improvements and suddenly had a useable pair of skates that worked like ice skates and could be used outdoors in the warm weather. They called their product Rollerblade® skates and formed a company called Rollerblade, Inc.

Rollerblade® are the most recognized brand of in-line skates. The word Rollerblade® is a registered trademark of the Minneapolis-based American Sports Training Corporation (the company bought Rollerblade, Inc. from the Olson's in 1986). Rollerblade® skates cost between $100 and $400. Rollerblade® supplies skates for the U.S. Ski Team, the U.S. Biathlon Ski Team, the U.S. Disabled Ski Team, and the Boston Bruins— all of whom use the skates for training.

Buying the Right Skates

The type of skating you plan on doing will determine which type of in-line skates you buy. If you are looking for a good workout, you will want a more expensive, high-performance skate. If you just want to go for a leisurely skate, a less expensive model will do.

It's important to buy skates that fit. When you try on a pair of in-line skates, make sure you wear the socks you will use when skating. (Never buy skates without trying them on). The best socks are medium-weight athletic, or padded athletic socks. They absorb moisture and prevent blisters. Avoid using heavy cotton socks. They won't keep your feet dry and will cause foot problems.

Once you put on the skates, lace them firmly. Stand with your knees straight. Your toes should barely touch the front of the boot. If your toes feel cramped or if there is too much room, try another size. Now bend your knees. Your toes should slip back from the front of the boot. If your toes are still touching, the boot is too small.

Now that you have the right size boot in your price range, try to find one with the best ventilation. Many boots are made of solid plastic and don't allow the foot to breathe.

This causes heat and moisture buildup, and makes skating uncomfortable. Skates with vents are much lighter and faster than those without vents.

Look for a skate with a hinged cuff at the top of the skate. A hinged cuff allows flexible movement when you lean forward on your skates. It also give you a better and more comfortable fit.

The inside of the boot should have a padded foot bed. This absorbs shock and supports your arches. Foam liners are also available. They give you added comfort, and protect your feet from the hard outer shell of the boot.

The wheels are another part of an in-line skate that you should consider carefully. Most in-line skates come with four wheels. If you have small feet, your skate will probably have three wheels. Racers will want a boot that has five wheels. Five wheels provide more speed than the four-wheel models. If you're just starting

out, however, a four-wheel skate is recommended.

A good skate has a rigid wheel frame made
of nylon and fiberglass. This gives you a
stable ride. Grab the frame and try to twist it.
If you notice movement, the frame is too
flexible and won't give you a stable ride.

Taking Care of Your In-Line Skates

Most in-line skates are easy to care for. All
you need to do is wipe them occasionally
with a damp cloth.

After a long period of use, you may notice
that the wheels are wearing on one side. If
they are, it's time to rotate them.

Use the Allen and socket wrenches that come
with the skates to loosen the wheels. Take
the front wheel and place it in the third-
wheel position. The third wheel now becomes the front wheel. Take the second

wheel and place it in the back. The back wheel now becomes the second wheel. Make sure you turn each wheel so that the worn edge is facing outward. Now tighten the wheels. If they don't spin freely, loosen them slightly.

Sometimes the wheels need replacing. If you feel yourself dragging along, it's probably because the wheels are too worn. A new set of wheels can be purchased at most athletic stores that sell in-line skates.

The brake in the back of the right boot also needs replacing from time to time. When you find yourself tilting your right skate at a severe angle in order to stop, replace the brake. Most in-line skate manufacturers include an extra brake with each pair of skates. Otherwise, you can buy a new one at an athletic store. Use the Allen wrench provided by the skate manufacturer to remove the old brake. Once the new one is on, make sure it's tight.

Get into the habit of checking your skates before each use—especially the wheels. Spin them to see if they rotate freely. Wiggle the wheels and the brake to make sure they're secure. And make sure your laces aren't worn or frayed.

Protective Gear

Protective gear is recommended for all in-line skaters—especially for beginners. Wrist guards, knee and elbow pads, and a helmet will give you all the protection you need and most likely save you from a visit to the doctor's office if you should fall. You can buy this equipment at most athletic stores.

Ready to Roll

It's true that if you know how to ice skate, you can probably learn to use in-line skates fairly quickly. But don't assume they are the same, because they're not. It's always a good idea to practice, avoid crowds and hills, and take things slow when learning to "blade."

The best place to learn balance is on the grass. You will be able to practice standing on your skates without moving. Lace your skates snugly, then slowly stand. Point your skates slightly outward and carefully walk forward. This is the basic skating motion.

Once you feel comfortable and in control of your walking, try running. Once you can run on your skates, jump back and forth from skate to skate. If you find that you can transfer your balance from one foot to the other—a basic skating maneuver—you are ready to roll on the pavement.

Find a smooth, dry, flat, and clean surface on which to practice. In-line skates do not work well on wet or dirty pavement. Make sure there is no traffic around to get in the way. An empty playground, parking lot, or tennis court will work fine. (Never attempt to skate on terrain that is too difficult for you).

Keep your weight on the balls of your feet and your knees bent. This keeps your weight forward for good balance. Keeping your hands slightly in front of you will also give you good balance.

Push off with one skate as far as possible. All your weight should be on the skate beneath you. Bring the other skate back, shift your weight to the other skate, then push out with the opposite skate. Go slowly and practice control and maintaining your balance. You can work on increasing your speed later.

Stops

Stopping is the most important part of in-line skating. Stopping always begins before you get out of control—not after. If you sense that you're about to lose control, it's time to slow down and stop.

There are several ways to stop when wearing in-line skates. The first is stopping with the heel brake (usually located on the back of the right boot). Lean slightly forward and extend your right leg forward so the heel brake drags the ground. Apply pressure to the brake by tilting your skate upward and bending your right knee. This will place your weight forward. The more weight you apply, the quicker you will stop.

Another stopping maneuver is the T-stop. Keep your knees bent with one skate pointing forward. Lift one skate and place it behind you, turning it outward in a "T" position. Now drag that skate's wheels on the ground and press downward. This maneuver will slow you down faster than using the break because you're dragging all your wheels (usually four) instead of one brake. Don't worry about wearing down the wheels. They're designed to take the punishment.

A third way to stop is to slow down—then perform a 360-degree turn with your skates pointed outward. This is an advanced maneuver that should be attempted only by experienced skaters.

Yet another advanced—and difficult—stopping technique is the power stop. Turn your front foot sideways at a very sharp angle and drag the wheels. *Power stops should not be attempted without instruction from an experienced blader.* Without the proper technique, you run the risk of turning an ankle.

Sometimes you will find yourself in a situation where none of the above stopping techniques will work—especially when someone suddenly jumps in front of you while you're on a narrow skating path. If you need to get out of the way, veer off onto the grass.

Once your skates catch the grass, they will stop. To avoid tumbling, run onto the grass until you're in control.

Turns

To turn in-line skates, you must be able to place your weight on the inside edges of the wheels.

To turn left, bend your knees and place your weight on the inside edge of your right skate. As you begin to turn, your left skate will follow in line. To turn right, bend your knees and place your weight on the inside edge of your left skate.

Experienced bladers will want to try a more advanced type of turn called the *crossover*. A crossover turn will allow you to keep your speed at a certain level while you turn.

Crossover turns require you to shift your weight completely from one skate to the other. To turn left, bend your knees and place all your weight on the left skate. Lift your right leg and cross it over the left leg. Shift your weight to the right skate and bring the left skate forward. Place your weight on the left skate. To continue turning, cross the right foot over the left and repeat the entire process.

To turn right, bend your knees and place all your weight on the right skate. Lift your left leg and cross it over the right leg. Shift your weight to the left skate and bring the right skate forward. Place your weight on the left skate. To continue turning, cross the right foot over the left and repeat the entire process.

Skating Backwards

Skating backwards is not as difficult as it looks. All you need is a little practice and confidence.

Find a flat surface—and make sure no one is behind you. Bend your knees and extend your hands forward. Point your skates slightly inward and keep your knees together. Push on the inside edges of the wheels. The skates will begin to spread outward. Once they are at shoulder width, turn your heels inward and bring the skates to the starting position. Repeat the process to build momentum. The harder you push, the faster you will go.

Once you have mastered skating backwards, you may want to learn backward crossovers. Begin by skating backwards until you've reached a comfortable speed. With your arms outstretched, place your weight on the back outer edge of the left skate. Cross the right skate over the left. Lift the left skate and place it in the spot the right skate had been. Repeat the process for a full turn.

When skating and turning backwards, always be aware of people around you. Never attempt backward maneuvers unless you have practiced them and feel comfortable.

Conditioning

Before you attempt any sporting activity, it is a good idea to prepare yourself by warming up properly. When you skip a warm-up routine, you run the risk of injury.

The best way to warm up is to skate at a slow pace for the first five minutes. Don't do stretching exercises before you skate. You run the risk of muscle tear.

When you're done skating for the day, take five minutes to cool down by skating at a slow pace. Afterwards, you can stretch. Your muscles are warm and won't tear as easily.

Where to Skate

If you are a beginner, empty parking lots, playgrounds, and driveways are the best places to practice. When you're ready to venture out, be selective of your skating area.

The streets might be tempting. But streets are not a good place to blade. Most streets are paved with a rough asphalt, and you'll find the vibration annoying and difficult. Besides, there are always cars to watch out for. Sidewalks are also tempting. But many sidewalks have cracks and bumps, and will make your skating difficult.

Many cities and towns have parks with smooth paved paths. These are ideal for blading. If you find a path, always be careful of others—and always be in control. You will have to share the path with pedestrians and bikers.

Don't attempt to skate on a rainy day. The wheels of your in-line skates are made of a very hard rubber and won't grip a wet surface. You will slip and fall, and run the risk of injury. If you happen to skate through a puddle, coast along the dry path until your wheels are dry again. Then resume your skating. If your skates get very wet, stop and dry them off.

You should also avoid skating through dirt and stones. The wheels of your skates will not turn on these surfaces, and you might tumble. And watch out for cracks in the pavement. If you catch your skate in a crack, you will fall.

In some cities where blading is popular, there are areas where in-line skating is restricted or limited. Watch for the signs, and always obey the rules. This will make the paths safer for everyone.

Extreme Skating

When you have mastered stopping, crossover turns, and backwards skating, you may want to try an aggressive form of blading called "extreme skating." Extreme skating involves jumps, stair riding, wall riding, and downhill skating.

Extreme skating should only be attempted after
you've had lots of training and practice.

The number one rule of extreme skating is this: Never attempt a stunt unless you feel in control and have practiced the maneuver. Attempting a stunt without practice isn't very smart—and you run the risk of serious injury.

Jumping is the first skill you should master because it forms the basis of all other stunts. Your first jump should be over something very small—like a crack in the pavement.

Build up speed before you attempt a jump. This will make the jump easier. As you approach the object, keep your feet together. Bend your knees and get into a crouched position, keeping the hands forward for better balance.

When you reach the object you are jumping, spring off the ground and pull your knees to your chest. Always keep your eyes forward, not down. When you land, place one foot slightly ahead of the other and land on your strong foot first (usually the back foot). Stride forward after you've completed the jump.

Stair riding is another popular form of extreme skating. The best way to learn is to find a set of stairs with a railing. As you hold onto the railing, try gliding over a few stairs. Bend your knees and place your strong foot forward, keeping your skates about six inches apart. One hand should be in front of you. Keep your weight back and your wheels straight. As you bounce down the stairs, let your back skate trail behind. Once you feel comfortable, try to skate down the stairs without using the rail.

Wall riding is a simple maneuver. Build up some speed as you approach the wall at an angle. When you reach the wall, touch it with one hand and spring off the outside skate. Place the inside skate on the wall and let the outside skate trail behind. Then land firmly on the outside skate as the inside skate follows.

Curb jumping is a necessity for those who blade on the streets. It is different than a regular jump because you use the top of the curb for launching.

Building speed, approach the top of the curb head-on with knees bent. When you reach the curb, simply glide over it. Because the curb is elevated, it will launch you. Then land on your strong foot.

Hill riding presents two different challenges. Getting up the hill is easy but takes a certain amount of strength. Use short strides so you don't get tired too quickly. And don't bend too much. Keep your weight on the balls of your feet and your back straight.

Coming down a hill requires control, style, and common sense. Never go down a hill that seems too steep for you. Skate with your weight forward and your body crouched. For added balance and control, keep one skate slightly ahead of the other and your arms still. Always keep your eyes forward.

If you feel yourself going too fast, start braking. Don't wait until you are out of control. If you can't stop and are losing control, you will have to begin a safe fall. Look for a soft area to land, preferably in the grass. Fall to one side, tucking your shoulder and head. Then roll or tumble. If you're wearing protective gear, you should come out of the fall with only a bruised ego.

If you reach a hill that's just too steep, take off your skates and climb or descend it. Don't be foolish by tackling a hill that you can't handle.

In-Line Hockey

You can also play hockey on in-line skates. Find a vacant parking lot to use as a rink. Make sure you tape the blade of your stick so it won't get worn out by the pavement. You can also use plastic hockey sticks. For a puck, try a tennis ball. A plastic puck also works well.

Some parks provide hockey nets for in-line skaters. If nets aren't available, use some

In-line hockey is faced-paced summer fun!

rocks, shoes, or scraps of wood to mark the goals. Then drop the puck and have fun!

A Final Word

Organized competition blading is still relatively new. But as the popularity of the sport continues to grow, so will the number of competitions. If you want to find out more about these competitions, call 1-800-255-RISA (Rollerblade® In-Line Skate Association).

In-line skating is an exciting and rewarding sports activity that can be enjoyed for many months of the year. To get the most out of the sport, practice your skating techniques, stay in control, and always exercise safety and caution.

GLOSSARY

- Crossover turn—an advanced turning technique in which the left and right skates are crossed over each other for faster turns.

- Curb jumping—an extreme skating style that uses curbs for jumps.

- Extreme skating—an advanced and aggressive form of in-line skating that uses stunts and tricks.

- Heel brake—the rubber stopper located on the heel of the right skate.

- Hill riding—an extreme skating style that takes the skater safely up and down a hill.

- Hinged cuff—the flexible top of the skate.

- In-line skates—roller skates with wheels that are aligned one behind another in a single line.

- Polyurethane—a very strong and durable plastic.

- Power stop—a difficult and advanced stopping maneuver in which the front skate is pointed sharply to the side and dragged.

- Stair riding—an extreme skating style that takes the skater down a set of stairs.

•T-stop—a stopping maneuver in which one skate is pointed sideways and dragged behind the skater.

•Wall riding—an extreme skating style that takes the skater across a wall.